Inculturation:

The Eucharist in Africa

by Phillip Tovey

Assistant Curate, Beaconsfield Team Ministry

THE ALCUIN CLUB and the GROUP FOR RENEWAL OF WORSHIP (GROW)

The Alcuin Club, which exists to promote the study of Christian liturgy in general and of Anglican liturgy in particular, traditionally published a single volume annually for its members. This ceased in 1986. Similarly, GROW was responsible from 1975 to 1986 for the quarterly 'Grove Liturgical Studies'. Since the beginning of 1987 the two have sponsored a Joint Editorial Board to produce quarterly 'Joint Liturgical Studies'. Full details of the current series of Joint Liturgical Studies are set out in the end-pages of this Study.

THE COVER PICTURE
is by Liz Robins following an idea by the author

First Impression September 1988
ISSN 0951-2667
ISBN 1 85174 091 0

GROVE BOOKS LIMITED
Bramcote   Nottingham   NG9 3DS

CONTENTS

ACKNOWLEDGEMENTS

My thanks go to the staff and students of Archbishop Janani Luwum Theological College, Gulu, Uganda, where I taught worship 1983-1985 as a rather raw mission partner. In fact this monograph tries to answer one of the examination questions that I set! Thanks also to Dr. Douglas Davies of Nottingham University who guided me in my research. Any mistakes however are all mine. Finally my thanks to those who encouraged me in the research and to John Waller and Michael Vasey who were kind enough to read the manuscript.

The Kenyan draft material in the Appendix is reprinted by kind permission of Dr. David Gitari, Bishop of Mount Kenya East, and chairman of the CPK Liturgical Committee.

1. Worship and Culture

Inculturation may seem another formidable word used by those who wish to cloud reality with a fog of incomprehensible terms. As such it can operate as a discouragement to those whose lives are directly affected each day by the problem, and can inhibit them from developing a critical awareness of their experience. But what is inculturation? Should it be looked at as a problem? Perhaps one way to understanding it is to examine the modern missionary movement and the results of this on the worship of the churches in the 'mission field'. As my own experience and study is limited to Africa, I shall restrict my examples to that continent. Also, rather than deal with the multiplicity of rites associated with the church, I shall confine the discussion to the eucharist, the central Christian ritual.

The missionary societies, in preaching the gospel to the Africans, tended to export the worship of the parent body, either in exactly the same form, or in the form that was seen to be ideal. Thus in Uganda the first missionaries began by translating parts of the Bible and the Book of Common Prayer. Together these two books formed the gospel as received. Hymns were from *Ancient and Modern*, and canticles were chanted in the Anglican way. In areas not evangelized by CMS the tendency was to provide a liturgy in keeping with the different ideals of the particular missionary society. Thus the Zanzibar Rite, developed in the UMCA area, was an adaptation of Cranmer's 1549 service in a more catholic direction.[1] Anglicanism and most other missions exported worship patterns lock stock and barrel, and perhaps this was inevitable. Although there were examples to the contrary, the prevailing attitude to African culture is expressed in the first line of the hymn 'Far far away in heathen darkness dwelling'—Africans lived in heathen darkness. As their religion penetrated all parts of their society, what was needed was to build a new Christian culture in Africa. Therefore the school became one of the major means of evangelism, for it removed children from their culture and put them in a new environment in which they could be civilized and Christianized.[2] If the Africans were in heathen darkness, then there was no reason to be sensitive to their culture. Missionaries had come to preach rather than to listen. Thus today on travelling to the villages in Uganda (for one example) it is possible to find Morning Prayer done in a traditional English Anglican way—a disappointment if one is looking for a vibrant African way of worship.

It is perhaps this disappointment that opens up the question of inculturation. Inculturation is seen as the transformation of the worship of the African Church to make it a more authentic expression of African Christianity. It is an elusive subject which can be seen in the complex of terms that has been used to describe

[1] B. Wigan, *The Liturgy in English* (OUP, London, [2]1962), pp.162-165.
[2] Hence secondary education occurs primarily in boarding schools.

it, adaptation, incarnation, indigenization contextualization.[1] Perhaps it is easiest to see it as one part of the wider discussion of the relationship between worship and culture. Due to the export of a system of worship, there is a sense that the worship does not fit. It does not make the worshipper 'feel at home'. Inculturation is the process of change by which this alienation is destroyed.

The objection can be raised that the study of inculturation is another form of imperialism. However this study does not attempt to make prescriptive comments about what churches in Africa should do in worship. Inculturation is not a subject to which there are answers as such but rather it is a process that occurs in all societies. The exported system can be from the past as much as from another culture. Indeed for some their own past is as foreign to them as another part of the world. The object here is to examine different examples of inculturation in order to understand some of the possibilities and problems.

The relationship between worship and culture is complex and there are a number of approaches that could be made. One way is to take the important category of 'symbol' and through it to examine inculturation in an interdisciplinary context. Symbol has been important to theologians and to anthropologists[2] and by viewing the eucharist as a symbol the discussion of inculturation can be elucidated.

This monograph will therefore begin by examining some of the approaches to symbol of different theologians and anthropologists. This does not attempt to be an exhaustive survey, rather it is an eclectic look at models drawn from both disciplines as they relate to the concrete problem of inculturation. Any interdisciplinary study may appear to fall between two stools and thus lack rigour. However this approach is based on the profound truth of Calvin that there are two parts to our wisdom, the knowledge of ourselves and the knowledge of God.[3] Anthropology, when scientifically based, can provide a knowledge of ourselves in the cultural context. Theology seeks the knowledge of God. But such statements are simplistic, for the reverse is also true. The knowledge of God can come through a greater understanding of the human world in which we live, and a deeper knowledge of man can be the result of the study of theology.[4] It is the interrelationship of the two forms of knowledge and at times their seeming incompatibility that is the basis of this Study. Rather than being a theoretical study seeking to look at the theology of culture or at the relationship between two academic disciplines, the bulk of this Study will examine particular examples drawn both from the Mission Churches and from African Independent Churches.

---

[1] G. A. Arbuckle, 'Inculturation not Adaptation: Time to change terminology' in *Worship*, 60 (1986), 511-520: A. A. R, Crollius, 'What is so new about Inculturation? A concept and its implications' in *Gregorianum*, 59 (1978), 721-738.

[2] F. W. Dillistone, *The Power of Symbols* (SCM, London, 1986).

[3] J. Calvin, *Institutes*, 1:1:1.

[4] J. Macquarrie, 'The Anthropological Approach to Theology' in *Heythrop Journal*, 25 (1984), 273-287.

2. Eucharist as Symbol

Inculturation has arisen in the present debate as a result of the modern missionary movement. But this is not to say that it has not been a longstanding problem. The Chinese rites controversy was an earlier discussion of the subject in the Roman Catholic Church.[1] It was also a question for the early church.[2] There are constant adaptations of the way a liturgy is enacted and even those who have a timeless liturgy that remains unchanged may have departed quite considerably from the way the rubrics intended. For example even the staunchest supporters of the Prayer Book had by the twentieth century dropped the use of Commination, the Athanasian Creed, and the exhortations in the Lord's Supper. In some sense the tradition of usage is an adaptation of the liturgy. But inculturation is usually reserved for more major changes, often of a cross-cultural nature. Such liturgical relocation may be because of missionary work, the movement of the gospel from one culture to another, or because of culture change in a particular culture. The Alternative Service Book could be seen as an inculturation of the tradition of the Church of England to the twentieth century. Thus the question of inculturation is not merely a question for the churches outside the traditional 'sending churches'. It is not a problem for them alone, but for us all.

Worship both in style and content interacts with changes in the culture in which it exists. The Reformation was a major upheaval in the worship of the Western Church, as it responded to new ideas. The Liturgical Movement has also been of great significance for most Western Churches and has resulted in the transformation of worship. This movement has had the strongest influence in Africa through the Roman Catholic Church, which has both vernacularized and reformed the liturgy as a result of the Second Vatican council. This council also encouraged the adaptation of worship to local culture.[3]

The study of worship as a symbol opens up a field of common interest for both theologians and anthropologists. The literature on symbol is vast, but there is little applying it to problems of the cross-cultural transference of a symbol. Before the theoretical positions of a number of anthropologists and theologians are examined, perhaps it is worth looking at one particular case to show the problems that can arise with the exporting of a particular rite.

Mbiti gives a wonderful example of the difficulties of the cross-cultural transference of the eucharist with reference to his own tribe.[4] The Africa Inland Mission were very cautious about the eucharistic discipline. The service always

[1] G. H. Dunne, *Generation of Giants* (University of Notre Dame Press, Notre Dame, Indiana, 1962): A. H. Rowthbotham, *Missionary and Mandarin, The Jesuits at the court of China* (University of California Press, Berkeley and Los Angeles, 1942).

[2] A. J. Chupungco, 'Greco-Roman Culture and Liturgical Adaptation' in *Notitiae*, 15 (1979), 202-218.

[3] Sacrosanctum Concilium § 37-40.

[4] J. Mbiti, *New Testament Eschatology in an African Background* (OUP, Lodnon, 1971), pp.91-126.

contained a reading from 1 Corinthians 11 including the warning verses 27-32. The Akamba tend to think in concrete ways and tend to have a 'magical' view of the world, therefore the reading of this passage was heard by them to give a magical nature to the eucharist similar to their own religious traditions. Those who eat unworthily will receive a curse and not a blessing. The result was that the missionaries were heard to be 'medieval' in their sacramental theology whereas in fact this was the exact opposite of what they were trying to convey. The issue here is not only of cultural horizons and the role of pre-understanding in the interpretation of scripture, but also of cultural apprehension of symbol and of a conflict in approaches to the eucharistic rite. This brings us to the work of Mary Douglas.

MARY DOUGLAS

Mary Douglas has argued strongly for the link between culture, cosmology and symbols.[1] Social action and choice contain implicit meanings. Thus a link exists between action, belief, and social structure. A model is developed with two parameters, those of grid and group. The difficulty of constructing a model that links culture, cosmology, and symbols, is such that her model is refined in the different editions of the book. This can easily lead to misunderstandings, but careful analysis of the work of Douglas can be fruitful in the context of an exploration of inculturation.

Starting from the work of Basil Bernstein, Mary Douglas utilizes a linguistic analogy for her understanding of a symbol. Restricted linguistic codes are found in groups where roles, values, and assumptions, are clearly defined and regulated. The code is there not only for communication but also for control. A restricted code is not only the particular jargon of the group but also the control of the individual by the use of the code. Likewise symbols condense the values of a particular society. They operate as a shorthand expressing values, norms, assumptions, and interpretations, of a group. The eucharist therefore has much to say about the centrality of Jesus in the interpretation of life for a community, and of the importance of the last events in the life of Christ, not least his death on the cross. Symbols both express group values and enforce a particular interpretation. Thus various behaviour-patterns and beliefs are required, if one is allowed to participate in the communion rite. When a particular interpretation is expressed and enforced, the symbols are said to be strongly condensed. When the control is weak and there is openness to personal interpretation, then the symbol is diffuse.

From this analysis of codes two parameters are developed, grid and group. Group is the experience of social bonding that enables a system of shared values. There are various factors in group. Is it a temporary or permanent group? Is it inclusive or exclusive? Is there a hierarchy in it or is it decentralized? All of these are group factors that influence the pattern of social bonding. Groups can therefore be strong or weak. With weak group bonding the individual is able to be self-assertive. Strong group bonding however means that the group concerns prevail over the individual.

---

[1] M. Douglas, *Natural Symbols, Explorations in Cosmology* (Penguin Books, Harmondsworth, 1970, 1973).

Grid is the control of the system of classification of the group. This classification entails an implicit cosmology, and thus grid is about the control of cosmologies. Sex roles, age roles, and charismatic leadership, influence the grid power. Strong grid means that the corporate classification prevails over the individual. Weak grid enables the possibility of private classification.

From this analysis Mary Douglas develops a model of different cultures and thus of their cosmology and symbol systems.

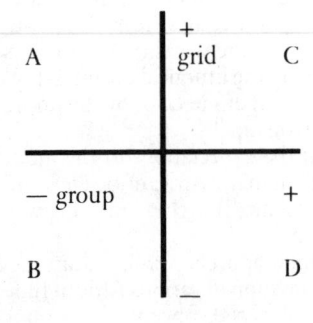

There are four types of culture:
A—where grid is strong and group is weak. This is exemplified in millennial or revival movements.
B—where grid and group are weak, for example modern permissive, pluralist society.
C—where grid and group are strong, for example the tribal agricultural societies in Africa.
D—where grid is weak but group is strong, for example nomadic tribal society.

Each of these societies has a different apprehension of symbols. We might view a society in type C as much more ritualistic than our own. On the other hand a weakening in the grid and group parameter might lead to a discussion of the powerlessness of symbols.

The missionary movement led to the transference of a symbol system, for example the Book of Common Prayer, from one culture to another. In the case of Anglican missions to Africa the transfer is from a society with weaker group and grid, industrial England, to one of stronger group and grid, tribal Africa. This almost inevitably leads to a sense that the symbol system as received does not fit, not only because the theological agenda set in the service book reflect the historical concerns of another society, but also because the apprehension of symbols by that other society differs. The grid group model suggests that those who live in societies with weak grid and group, type B, have a weak apprehension of symbol compared to those to strong grid group cultures, type C. To adapt Douglas, the colour-blind signalmen (the missionaries) were trying to teach the train drivers (the Africans) about the signals. Africans in tribal society are familiar with the use of symbols. It was the missionaries who had inherited the traditions of the Reformation who found them difficult. Any comments about another culture are made from within one's own particular cultural constraints, but it is possible at this point to utilize some personal observations. One thing that struck me was the incipient sacramentalism of the church in Uganda There seemed to be few of our inhibitions about symbols. Marriage and ordination were called sacraments, even in the 'low church' Church of Uganda. Ministers were happily called priests. This is to be expected from Douglas' model, for stronger grid group societies have a greater apprehension of, and less inhibitions about, symbols. A second observation comes from B. Idowu who comments on the attractiveness of Roman Catholic worship, even if it is a foreign package:

'What seems to cover up the liturgical unsuitability in their own set up is the fact that it is heavily compensated for by the impressive paraphernalia of a dramatic ritualistic worship.'[1]

This again seems to fit the expectations of the model. The apprehension of symbol was stronger both in many African societies and in the Roman Catholic Church than in the Protestant Churches, and this was a point of contact and attention to many Africans.

The relation of symbolic apprehension, culture and the eucharist will be returned to with the examination of various African Independent Churches. The next step however is to look at the concept of a symbol more closely and relate this to the eucharist.

VICTOR TURNER

Turner did his fieldwork agmong the Ndembu in Zambia. Later in life he applied his studies to his own tradition, that of Roman Catholicism. He saw symbol as a subdivision of ritual. Ritual is 'prescribed formal behaviour for occasions not given over to technological routine, having reference to beliefs in mystical (or non-empirical) beings or powers'.[2] The smallest unit of ritual behaviour is the symbol. It may be associated with any object, activity, relationship, word, gesture, or spatial arrangement in a ritual situation. Turner distinguishes between signs and symbols. Signs have only one referant and therefore only one meaning. Symbols on the other hand condense many values, ideas and concepts. Thus they refer to many things, and have a multiplicity of meanings associated with them. Symbols are 'storage units, into which are packed the maximum amount of information . . . they can be regarded as multi-faceted mnemonics, each facet corresponding to a specific cluster of values, norms, beliefs, sentiments, social roles, and relationships'.[3] Thus the eucharist not only condenses values of the importance of the death of Christ to a particular community, but also talks of the organization of that community (in who is allowed to lead the eucharist), of their social values (through the moral restrictions on participants), of beliefs (expressed in the words used in the service), and of their relationships with other groups (through policies of intercommunion).

---

[1] B. Idowu, *Towards an Indigenous Church* (OUP, London and Ibadan, 1975), p.28.
[2] V. Turner, *The Drums of Affliction* (OUP, Oxford, 1968), p.15.
[3] *ibid.*, p.1.

Turner saw that some symbols are more important in a ritual than others. These dominant symbols are more stable in meaning and preside over the whole ritual. Thus the bread and the wine, the body and blood of Christ, are dominant in the eucharist. Other symbols support these dominant symbols but are of secondary importance, for example the posture in receiving the elements, the commixture, censing of the elements, the position of the altar-table.

The dominant symbol has two poles of meaning, the ideological and the orectic (or sensory). The ideological pole has a cluster of beliefs, values, norms, principles of social organization attached to it. This multi-vocality with regard to the eucharist can be seen in the interpretative framework given to the symbol in the scriptures, communion in Christ, eschatological feast, living bread, manna, cup of salvation, and of the different approaches made by different churches, fellowship meal, offering, sacrifice. Turner's comment that symbols are multi-vocal is important for it illuminates some aspects of eucharistic debate. In that the eucharist condenses many values and beliefs, part of the process of debate is of a discussion of the interpretation of particular beliefs and of the ranking of these beliefs within the context of the whole. Such multi-vocality also raises the question as to the extent to which definition of a symbol is possible, for if there is a complex of meanings to a symbol, can there be only one interpretation? Is this not trying to turn a symbol into a sign? Will not the multi-vocality of the symbol undermine any attempt of over-definition?

The other pole of meaning is the orectic pole, which is associated with the outward form of the symbol. Those from some Protestant traditions may not regard the actual form of the eucharist as very important, but in Africa this can be a difficult issue. A bottle of wine may cost a parish more than the collection for three months (the experience in the villages in the part of northern Uganda where I was working). In this economic climate is the use of wine important? Are local substitutes valid? If banana wine is used, does it matter that it is not red? Pragmatism may seem to be the approach of some, but this position is debatable.

This question has produced a variety of approaches. Cyprian argued that we must do what Jesus did.[1] The eleventh century saw a serious dispute between the Eastern Church and the West over the form of the eucharist.[2] The Ethiopian Orthodox Church prepares the bread and wine in a special house, Bethlehem, next to the church. Wine is made from imported raisins that are then steeped in water. Early travellers to Ethiopia commented on the strange nature of the wine used for the eucharist, and the Vatican in 1706 declared that wine prepared in this way was invalid. Uzukwu has argued that the important concept in the form used is that of 'daily bread' and so, as bread and wine reflect a Mediterranean form of agriculture, Africanization of the elements would open the possibility of

---

[1] Cyprian Epistle LXII. 'To Caecilius on the sacrament and the cup of the Lord', in *Writings of the Ante-Nicene Fathers Vol. 5,* edited by A. Roberts and J. Donaldson (Eerdmans, Grand Rapids, 1957) pp.358-364.

[2] J. H. Erikson, 'Leavened and Unleavened: Some Theological Implications of the Schism of 1054' in *St. Vladimir's Theological Quarterly,* 14 (1970), 156-176.

the use of maize cake and banana wine (with local variations).[1] Unfortunately the higher authorities in the Roman Catholic Church do not agree. Bishop Dupont (diocese of Pala, Chad, 1973-1975) celebrated the eucharist using millet bread and millet beer due to difficulties of importing wine, and was subsequently relieved of office.

A diversity of matter is used in the churches of Africa. The debate that continues, indicates that orectic issues are on the agenda for the continent. The answers given as to what form should be used vary from the Roman Catholics, who have developed a distribution system for importing wheat and wine, to the Friends of the Holy Spirit in Machakos, who in the context of an evening fellowship meal used *kyavati* (a sort of thin local bread) and brown coffee with sugar distributed from one cup.

There are two other aspects of Turner's work that are important with reference to inculturation. The first is related to his concept of liminality. Drawing from the work of Van Gennep on initiation rites, Turner distinguishes three phases in initiation; preparation, limen, and reaggregation. The preparation is the separation of the individual or group from their every-day life. This may entail the physical separation of the group either through retreat into the bush, and or through their living apart in a house for the initiands. The liminal period is when the initiation process occurs and in which the norms of society are restructured for the individual through instruction, rituals and endurance tests. Symbols are often used to restructure initiands' beliefs and understanding of the tribe and the cosmos. The final phase is the reintegration of the initiands into the tribe, now as adults. This model has become well known and is applied to different rites of Christian worship. It is important to notice that essential to Turner's model is the social transformation of the individual. A boy may enter the circumcision rite as a boy, but he comes out of it as a man. The application of this model to the eucharist, however, is limited because the eucharist is not a rite of social transition.

Turner further applied this model to the history of a culture. He suggested that societies go through liminal periods and that in these times there is a restructuring of that culture and the production of new symbols. It is in the limen, the transitional phase, that there is the birth of symbols, for the limen is the place of anti-structure leading to new structure. The margin, a second important concept, is the edge of the present structure where there is also the possibility for change. These models need to be used carefully. One difficulty is in finding clear boundaries to delineate a liminal period. The 1960s may have been one such a period for the western world, but its boundaries are rather diffuse. The Second Vatican Council is a much better example, as it was a clear antistructure that led to the transformation of the Catholic Church. In the African setting the Independent Churches are more marginal than liminal. In these churches there is an ongoing dialogue with African culture, which is leading to the transformation of worship and the production of new symbols. The next chapter will look at the eucharist in some of these churches.

---

[1] E. E. Uzukwe, 'Food and Drink in Africa and the Christian Eucharist' in *AFER*, 72 (1980), 370-385.

Having briefly examined the anthropological approaches to symbol of Douglas and Turner we can gain further insights into symbol by turning to the theologians. Two areas will be studied: the theology of Paul Tillich, and the discussion surrounding the term *lex orandi lex credendi*.

PAUL TILLICH

Symbol is a primary category in the theology of Tillich, sacramental theology being only a subsection of his general approach. He reacted to people who used the langauge 'only a symbol'. To Tillich there was never 'only a symbol' or a 'mere symbol'. Symbols were of ultimate importance and the person who used such language about them had not come to understand their significance. He was critical of the sacramental tradition of Protestantism in that he saw the death of sacramental consciousness had led to the reduction of the sacramental dimension to one level, that of the sacrament of the word. He argued that the pressing need in the Protestant tradition was a rediscovery of the sacramental dimension.

Tillich posited four general characteristics of a symbol: figurative quality, perceptibility, innate power, and acceptability.[1] The figurative quality of the symbol relates to the fact that a symbol does not point to itself but to that which is symbolized. This he developed, when he made the distinction between sign and symbol. The perceptibility of the symbol is that the symbol makes perceptible something that is transcendent, intrinsically invisible or ideal, and through it the symbolized is made objective. The third characteristic is that the symbol has innate power. It is because of this innate power that Tillich can begin to talk of the birth and death of symbols. A symbol has a life independent of those who participate in it. Thus the eucharist in Africa can undergo a culture-shock in the process of its fitting into its new cultural context. The final characteristic, acceptability, points to the social rooting of symbols. They cannot be manufactured but must be acceptable to the culture in which they live. If they are no longer acceptable then they will die.

Tillich tried to distinguish between a 'sign' which points beyond itself, and a 'symbol' which both points beyond itself and also participates in that to which it points. This fundamental division in Tillich has come under heavy criticism. There seems to be little scope within his theology to be able to make such a distinction, for every relation is for Tillich a kind of participation. Also it is not clear what to 'participate in the reality' means.[2] Such criticisms are fundamental blows to the overall structure of Tillich's theology, but there are still important elements left to consider.

Tillich talked of the innate power of the matter. He wanted to say that the relationship between the symbolic matter and that which was symbolized was not arbitrary. This led to some very strange discussions as to the power of numbers and the nature of matter that may seem to verge on the pantheistic.[3]

---

[1] Tillich, P. 'The Religious Symbol', in F. W. Dillistone (ed.), *Myth and Symbol* (SPCK, London, 1966).

[2] W. L. Rowe, *Religious Symbols and God. A Philosophical Study of Tillich's Theology* (University of Chicago Press, Chicago and London, 1968).

[3] P. Tillich, *The Protestant Era* (Nisbet and Co. Ltd., London, 1951), ch. 7 'Nature and Sacrament', pp.105-125.

However this position of symbolic realism rejects the approach which makes the connection between the symbol and the thing symbolized totally arbitrary, for this would undermine any powerful link between the symbol and that to which it points. In this he parallels Turner, who from a different starting point elaborated the significance of the material pole of the symbol.

The life and death of symbols is perhaps more related to the issue of inculturation. Even in our own culture we are aware that symbols can become 'dark and dumb ceremonies'. As such they are dead and no longer open up our own consciousness or deeper levels of reality. They may remain fossilized, they may revive or they may die. Thus a whole gamut of symbols related to the eucharist died in the Reformation for the Protetant Churches. In the Church of England consignations, incense, vestments, processions of the blessed sacrament, lavabo, commingling and commixture, all of these symbols died, some rapidly and some more gradually. But at the same time other symbols were revived, not least communion through participation. The vision of the Reformers, to make this communion a frequent activity, was not acceptable in their culture and their desires remained frozen for many years as abstract rubrical assumptions. The Liturgical Movement in Protestantism picked up this desire and has been successful where the Reformers were not. It has also led to the revival of some signs that have long been dead, not least the Peace, which for some has become a very meaningful activity.

The birth and death of symbols is to some extent linked to their ability to open up levels of ultimate reality to a community. The Reformation was a time of the death of many symbols due to prophetic criticism of the church. But there was also the death of many symbols, that were in many ways neutral to criticism from the new Biblical theology. This suggests changes in the structure of society and its capacity of symbolic apprehension. Indeed the Reformation resulted in a range of approaches to symbol varying from hostility to ambivalence. The Book of Common Prayer, for example, resisted the abolition of all symbols (for example in the debates about wedding rings and the signing of the cross in baptism), but maintained the position that the bread put in your hands is the body of Christ (in the words of administration), even if a few pages later the body of Christ is said to be in heaven (in the black rubric)!

Tillich also discusses adequacy in relation to a symbol which relates to its ability to function in a two-edged way, in opening up levels of reality that would otherwise be closed to us and also in unlocking dimensions of our soul to the depths of human consciousness. In this process there is always a cultural component, and symbol will be alienated from a group if its expression is too bound with a foreign culture. Inculturation is the process of the removal of this alienation. It is a dynamic process that occurs in all cultures. Symbols are either becoming inculturated and speaking powerfully to the society or there is increasing alienation of the symbol. Symbols have the power to cross the cultural barriers in ways that humans do not. Few humans can ever integrate themselves fully into another culture so that they can totally relate to that culture. Even the most sympathetic are still reminded at times that they are foreign. Symbols can go beyond that and actually become the core of the culture. In the debate about the ASB there have been many criticisms, but few have complained that there has been the introduction of foreign symbols. Yet in Africa this is one of the chief criticisms of the Mission Churches, that the worship is not African.

The nature of symbols as developed by Paul Tillich throws further light on the question of inculturation. Symbols are born and die, and this may be the result of prophetic criticism. The adequacy of a particular symbols may include a cultural component to it, not least if the materials used for the symbol are foreign to the culture in which it has been introduced.

LEX ORANDI LEX CREDENDI

This epigram has been much debated in liturgical studies. In particular Alexander Schmemann and Aidan Kavanagh have both argued for the worship of the church as the starting point for theology. Theology is seen by Schmemann as 'a search for words and concepts adequate to and expressive of the living experience of the Church'.[1] He complains that theology has become autonomous, independent of the worship experience of the church, and this has led to the scholastic approach to liturgy which leads to the feeding back of categories into the liturgy such as causality, which are in origin conceptually independent of the worship experience. Schmemann would rather want to see the link of theology and liturgy as organic.

One of the problems with the work of Schemann is that there does not appear to be a clear enough definition of terms. At first it would seem that he is arguing that the liturgical experience should be the basis for theology, and that theologizing would occur as there is reflection on the event. Thus there would be, in the terms of Kavanagh, a distinction made between primary theology (as expressed in the liturgical event) and then secondary theology (reflection on that).[2] The question has to be raised as to the interrelationship between these two types of theology. Schmemann, in attacking the scholastic approach, rejects all feedback from secondary theology. Nor, as he states it, is liturgy a datum for theology. This then is to reject some of the processes of liturgical development in the west, not least the development of the eucharistic cultus, and the critical approach of the Reformation, both of which move from theology to worship. But Schmemann does not develop a clear relationship between theology and worship. Perhaps it is better to see worship and theology in a hermeneutical circle, and to suggest that the debate is over where the starting point of entering this circle is to be found. Schmemann and Kavanagh argue for the worship event as that point.

This debate is of importance in providing background for the study of inculturation. There is a feeling that there is something wrong in the worship event. It is not adequately expressing the African spiritual experience. This feeling was worldwide among Catholics and was expressed in Vatican II. The first document of that Council was on worship and it opened the possibility of the cultural adaptation of the liturgy. The Independent Churches have grown for

---

[1] A. Schmemann, 'Liturgy and Theology' in *Greek Orthodox Theological Review*, 17 (1972), p.90.

[2] A. Kavanagh, *On Liturgical Theology* (Pueblo, New York, 1984), pp.73-95.

many reasons, but one of their main concerns is to worship God in their own African way. Few Independent Churches are involved in the production of secondary theology. Most are content with their worship experience and the preaching which goes on in that. But as such they do not differ from many of those in the west who attend church.

Perhaps *lex orandi lex credendi* has become important in the west as a corrective to doctrinal dominance of liturgy. It also is supported by the development of existentialist philosophy, and the stress on the subjective experience. In the study of worship it tangentially connects with phenomenological approaches, and with those who want to begin with a sociological or anthropological analysis. It points to the worship event as the place for the beginning of reflection, and of the depth of this experience as critical to the life of the church.

EUCHARIST AND INCULTURATION

A monograph can only introduce a particular subject. The relationship of worship and culture is of necessity a complex one which will continue to be debated. However inculturation is both a process, unconsciously occurring in some churches, and also consciously perceived as a problem to be solved in others. Its root may be seen as the alienation of symbols as a result of cultural changes either through time or diffusion.

The following chapters look at the response of the churches in Africa to this problem. Africa is a continent undergoing tremendous change. Westernization has had a major impact and the old traditions have been weakened. The church is growing rapidly and the missionary movement has resulted in many overseas provinces indigenously led. Inculturation may in part be a reaction against the process of westernization, a clinging to the past. But that would seem to be only a partial analysis. It is more the digestion of the gospel and its coming to fruition in authentic African expression. It entails an agenda in the worship event which relates to the daily experience of the participants, and the use and apprehension of symbols that speak clearly in a particular context. It is not a problem for which there is one solution. Different churches have different responses, and the Independent Churches provide one point of departure.

3. African Independent Churches

The growth of the Independent Churches is one of the most significant aspects of the present flourishing of Christianity in Africa. Mbiti has declared that they are the truly indigenous churches of the continent, alongside the Ethiopian Orthodox Church.[1] The two are not unconnected in that the victory of the Ethiopians over the Italians encouraged Independent Churches, for Africans began to see that they could organize themselves and did not have to rely on white leadership. But the influence is symbolic, Independent Churches existed prior to that war, even before the stimulus of the Ethiopian victory.

The movement is very diverse and varies from small churches of only one congregation, to denominations with millions of members. The orthodoxy of the churches also varies from those that are within the mainstream of Christian tradition to some with their own Messiah. These churches have broken away from the Mission Churches for a number of reasons, not least in the colonial period because of a desire for African leadership, or more recently due to disagreements with leaders of the black-led Mission Churches, or the desire to develop a style of worship that is more African. There are break-away churches from the Roman Catholic Church, but the vast majority have parted from Protestant Churches, Anglican churches founded by CMS have been particuarly prone to schism.

The churches often worship without books and do not write theological works explaining their doctrine. However some do produce orders of service, and pamphlets explaining their theology. The examination of the eucharist in these churches will be within the context of the whole ritual system. The Church of the Lord (Aladura) is a Nigerian church founded in the 1930s and will be the first example studied. This will be followed by the Kimbanguist Church in Zaire.

THE CHURCH OF THE LORD (ALADURA)

The Church of the Lord is only one of a whole number of Aladura Churches existing in Nigeria, in West Africa generally, and even in Britain. The movement began with campaigns of evangelism, preaching and healing, under the influence of the flu epidemic of 1918 and American Pentecostalism. The Church of the Lord was the result of visions received by Josiah Oshitelu, a first-generation Christian, who was employed as a pupil-teacher in the Anglican Church and was being trained as a catechist. In 1925 his visions began, which he recorded, and in 1926 he was suspended by the Anglican Church. He devoted his time to prayer and preaching, married seven wives and founded the Church. He was a prophetic figure who emphasized the importance of spiritual healing.

The Church of the Lord has produced a number of booklets that explain their approach to worship. The rituals of the Church are a development of Anglican

---

[1] J. Mbiti, *African Religions and Philosophy* (Heinemann, Ibadan, Nairobi and London, 1969), pp.232-236.

worship, parts are direct from the Book of Common Prayer, others are adaptations of the Anglican liturgy and some new services are provided. Worship is of great importance to the Church and it is the inadequacy of Anglican worship that is seen as the justification for the formation of a new church.[1] The Church of the Lord rejects infant baptism, accepts polygamy, and gives great importance to symbols in worship.

Morning and evening prayer are daily activities. Fasting is strictly observed, particularly on Wednesdays and Fridays, and the Mission Churches are criticized for their laxity in this area. In Lent fasting is especially encouraged, there are special services and the litany is particularly used. This is a reworking of the Litany of the 1662 Book of Common Prayer, much simplified. The material has been reworded and reflects an African agenda. It is divided into three parts by the triple repetition of:

Priest: We use our mouths like a broom before Thee.
Cong.: **Good Lord, have mercy on us.**

This is accompanied by the prostration of the congregation, about which Turner comments that this is the traditional practice of humiliation and penance before a Yoruba king.[2] Some of the petitions reflect the concerns of the culture with regard to witchcraft:

Priest: From the attacks of wizards and witches.
Cong.: **Good Lord, deliver us . . .**
Priest: Over those who employ spirits against us.
Cong.: **Good Lord, give us victory.**
Priest: Over all bad and wicked juju-men.
Cong: **Good Lord, give us victory.**

There is also a strong apocalyptic section:

Priest: In the days of wars and the rumours of war.
Cong.: **Good Lord, deliver us . . .**
Priest: In the days that the moon shall be troubled and it shall become blood.
Cong.: **Good Lord, deliver us.**

This is an adaptation of the Book of Common Prayer both in style, with shorter petitions enabling greater responsorial participation, and in content, reflecting an African agenda of prayer concerns.

This Church has a variety of holy places. Firstly there is the village church or temple. Most are simple structures with the sanctuary railed off. This is a holy of holies which often contains a light wooden table with an altar cloth, a seven-branched candelabrum, some paper flowers, and a wooden cross. The lectern

---

[1] E. O. Adeleke Adejobi, *The Bible Speaks on the Church of the Lord* (Central Printing Press, Kamasi, 1950).

[2] H. W. Turner, *African Independent Church Vol. 2. The Life and Faith of the Church of the Lord (Aladura)* (Clarendon Press, Oxford, 1967), p.168.

and the table for the blessing of water are outside the sanctuary. God is believed to be specially present in the temple. Secondly, there is a special area attached to the church called the mercy ground. This is a holy place for prayer to which people may go before the service. Thirdly, there are home altars which often contain a cross, candle and Bible. Turner comments that there is precedent for this in Yoruba household shrines.[1] Fourthly, the city where the visions first took place, Ogere, is regarded as holy. It is not a place of pilgrimage, but a large cathedral is being built there. Fifthly, there is the holy hill of Mount Tabora to which is made a large pilgrimage every year.

A whole variety of symbols are used in the church. Members are expected to wear a white apparel as an 'emblem of purity and chastity Rev. 7.9'.[2] Candles are used and justified from Ex. 25.31. Palm leaves are used as 'emblems of victory . . . Rev. 7.9'.[3] An iron rod is used as a staff of office; it is 'a visible omen of the victory through Christ'.[4] A turban may be worn by some leaders according to Zec. 3.5. All manner of objects may be used in healing: handkerchiefs, oil, salt, water, clay, and incense. Two parts of the Bible have been particularly influential in the development of these symbols, the Old Testament and the book of Revelation. The introduction of a particular symbol has often come as the result of a vision.

Church services are not as static as those of the mission parent. Besides kneeling there are prostrations, kissing the Bible, clapping, shouting, use of the sign of the cross, anointing, laying on of hands, the sprinkling with holy Water, and usually at some point in the service there is dancing. Some of these uses are interpreted by Apostle Adejobi:

'Palm leaves are given and water sprinkled on people as a visible sign of sanctification as Moses sanctified the children of Israel with water and ointment. The blood of Jesus represented by water, we now apply as a super sanctifying and cleansing force.'[5]

Shoes are removed on entering the temple and there may be water provided to wash the feet.

There is a well developed hierarchy in the church. Among the men the pattern is as follows:

	Primate	
Apostle		Bishop
Rev. Apostle		Rev. Deacon
Senior Prophet		Senior Evangelist
Prophet		Evangelist
Acting Prophet		Captain
	Teacher	

---

[1] *Ibid.,* p.103.
[2] E. O. Adeleke Adejobi, *The Bible Speaks on the Church of the Lord,* p.4.
[3] *Ibid.,* p.4.
[4] E. O. S. Ade Adejobi, *The Observance and Practices of the Church of the Lord* (Peoples Star Press, Ibadan, n.d.) p.7.
[5] E. O. Adeleke Adejobi, *The Bible Speaks on the Church of the Lord,* p.8.

The two lines represent two different types of ministry, those with spiritual gifts and with pastoral gifts (preaching and administration). There are also six grades of women's ministry:

Rev. Mother
Rev. Deacon
Prophetess
Lady Evangelist
Lady Captain
Sister

All these ranks have their own particular vestments and their duties are carefully prescribed. Whereas in England there has been a reaction against rank and title, the African church finds that this is attractive, for it is in continuity with the traditional value of giving honour to the elders.

The use of 'Holy Words' is 'one of the most bizarre features of the Church of the Lord'.[1] Strange words are spoken, sung, and incorporated into the liturgy. There is no special relationship of these holy words to glossolalia; the church also allows the gift of tongues. The holy words are meaningless in themselves, in the sense that normal conversation cannot be conducted in them, but they do convey various suggestions to the church members. They are regarded as revelations from the Lord, a special gift from God. At the consecration in the communion the priest offers 19 holy words including Jehovah, Yaawaanniei, Yaawaarraa . . . Labieussas.

Water is a very important symbol in the church. Feet are washed on entering the church but its most important use is in healing. 'We make no use of medical aid besides the use of Holy Water.'[2] The church had its origins in the experience of the power of God in healing, that Christ was not only Saviour but also healer. This has led to a rejection of western medicine which for much of its history was in the hands of the missions. 'The Lord has provided and established this water for the Healing of all diseases, body and spirit. The water may be likened to the Ark amongst the children of Israel in those days provided for them for their redemption.'[3] This water is blessed towards the end of the service and taken away to be drunk or applied to the body.

Water is also used for purification. After the general confession, water is sprinkled on the people using a palm branch, which 'stands for an outward sign of that continuous cleansing pool which flows still in the blood of Jesus Christ. Lev. 8; Ez. 36.35'.[4] This practice also occurs at the confession in holy communion. Although water is sprinkled on a child at his or her naming, this should not be confused with baptism, as the church rejects infant baptism.

The catechism in the Book of Rituals follows the order of that of the Book of Common Prayer. However there are some major differences when it comes to the sacraments. There is no definition of a sacrament. The questions associated

---

[1] H. W. Turner, *African Independent Church Vol. 2* p.272.
[2] E. O. Adeleke Adejobi, *The Bible Speaks on the Church of the Lord,* p.8.
[3] *Ibid.,* p.5.
[4] E. O. S. Ade Adejobi, *The Observance and Practice of the Church of the Lord,* p.11.

with baptism explain the rejection of infant baptism (infants cannot confess). There is nothing about communion at all. Instead there is a section on the 'Water of Life'. 'What is required to drink the Water of Life? Self-examination'.[1] It would seem that holy water has taken on the function of the eucharist. This is compounded by the use of the image of the blood of Christ associated with holy water, as has been quoted above.

However there is a flexibility in doctrine and the catechism from Ghana has a section on the eucharist.[2] A sacrament is 'a sacred act instituted by Jesus Christ in which fixed and visible tokens connected with its word of promise God offers and gives us great spiritual blessing'.[3] There are two sacraments. Baptism has such power because of the word of God which is 'in and with the water'.[4] The Lord's Supper is also called the Sacrament of the Altar and the body and blood of Christ are eaten 'under the bread and the wine'.[5] The catechism explicitly rejects both the Catholic doctrine and the Reformed view, which it interprets in a Zwinglian way. However 'Real Presence' is affirmed and the benefit is seen as the forgiveness of sins. The last two questions are concerned with the worthiness of the communicant and the warning of 1 Corinthians 11.28-29 is expounded.

The order for holy communion in the Book of Rituals is as follows:
1 Sentence.
2 Rubric directing the unworthy not to participate.
3 Hymn—'I hunger and I thirst'.
4 Ps. 51 followed by a prayer of absolution.
5 Hymn—'Jesus, my Saviour, look on me.'
6 The Ten Commandments.
7 Pss. 65, 32, 130, with a prayer of absolution
8 Hymn—'There is a fountain filled with blood'.
   During the hymn holy water is sprinkled on everybody
9 Pronouncement of the absolution of sins.
10 Prayer of consecration. This includes the use of the 19 holy names and, 'Consecrate . . . all these vessels . . . and also the bread and the wine . . . that we may not be killed by them. Let the bread become changed to the flesh of Christ and this wine the blood of Jesus Christ . . . may we for ever live in Thee, Amen.'
11 The Narrative of Institution is read.
12 Hymn—'Come, the feast is ready.'
13 Distribution using the words of the Book of Common Prayer.
14 Hymn
15 Closing prayer
16 Benediction

---

[1] Church of the Lord. *Book of Rituals*, p.34.
[2] S. Krow, *99 Questions and Answers on the Church of Lord Doctrine*, (Accra, Ghana, 1961), questions 70-97.
[3] *Ibid.*, question 70.
[4] *Ibid.*, question 75.
[5] *Ibid.*, question 86.

The service is held at night, the atmosphere is subdued, there is no clapping. The people have to be clean to receive. The water for sprinkling is consecrated by the passing of the iron rod over the water and the hymn is often sung that includes the lines:

'What can wash away my stain?
Nothing but the blood of Jesus.'

The iron rod is also used in the consecration of the elements. Each of the elements is touched with the rod during the consecration prayer. The closing prayer often gives thanks for 'the power of life, healing, salvation, and eternal life given to us', and there is often an element of self-oblation.[1]

The origin of the rite is the Book of Common Prayer, but there have been some radical changes. An examination of three motifs in this service show the changes that have occurred.

Firstly, there is a stronger emphasis on purity. The first half of the service stresses the need for cleansing from sin. The Ten Commandments set standards. The psalms are penitential. There are three absolutions and this is sealed by the use of Holy Water. This in itself is seen as a symbol of the cleansing blood of Christ. The impure are not allowed to partake. The danger is that the rite becomes something only for the holy rather than the means of holiness.

Secondly there is a stronger emphasis on consecration. Much of the material of Cranmer which emphasizes praise (e.g. the Sursum Corda) and that which emphasizes the service as a holy meal (e.g. the prayer of humble access) has been omitted. The consecration prayer in Cranmer is a prayer for fruitful reception. The Church of the Lord has revised this into a prayer of consecration of the elements, 'Let this bread be changed into the flesh of Christ'.[2] Indeed the prayer begins with a prayer for the consecration of the vessels, which has more in common with the Ethiopian Orthodox Church than with Cranmer. This emphasis on consecration is associated with an embryonic doctrine of awe concerning the consecration. The rubrics direct that 'everybody shall kneel by the altar reverently and with awe and receive'.[3] Thus there is a stress on the fact of consecration. If the Book of Common Prayer had the ambiguity of calling the prayer the Prayer of Consecration while praying for fruitful reception, the Church of the Lord has developed a prayer of consecration that prays for consecration.

Thirdly, the words of Paul in 1 Corinthians 11.27-30 have a much stronger influence in this rite than in Cranmer. The prayer of consecration specifically asks that 'Thy children who shall partake thereof may suffer no stomach trouble thereby nor become ill through same, that we may not be killed by them'.[4] This supports Mbiti's assertion of these verses being interpreted in a 'magical' way.

---

[1] H. W. Turner, *African Independent Church Vol. 2*, p.208.
[2] Church of the Lord, *Book of Rituals* p.30.
[3] *Ibid.*. p.31.
[4] Church of the Lord, *Book of Rituals* p.30.

The eucharist may not be celebrated very frequently in the Church of the Lord, but this may reflect the older pattern of infrequent communion in the Mission Churches. It may also be a reflection of the difficulty of apprehending a symbol that relies on imported materials, in contrast to water that is universally available. A western eye may view the worship of the Church as an Anglican service that has been adapted in a Catholic-Pentecostal direction. This view is very much a western view. To the African it may seem that the service has been enriched with the addition of biblical symbols to produce a service in which to feel at home. The historical rejection of some symbols in worship, e.g. incense, may not be understood and so they are readily introduced. Indeed sometimes symbols were abolished in the Reformation because of associations with Catholicism rather than through any intrinsic rejection of the symbol. To the African such division may seem remote or even irrelevant. Traditions can be overcome in the context of a prophet who is speaking the word of the Lord to an African church.

Another example of an Independent Church will serve to enrich our understanding of some of the dynamics of this movement. Therefore this study can now turn to the Kimbanguist Church in Zaire, one of the largest Independent Churches, claiming a membership of some five million people.

THE KIMBANGUIST CHURCH

Simon Kimbangu was born in 1889.[1] He was blessed by a Baptist (BMS) missionary and was brought up by his aunt after the death of his parents. In 1915 he and his wife were baptized in the river Tombe and their marriage was solemnized in church. One night in the 'flu epidemic of 1918 Kimbangu heard a call from God to lead the church. He fled to Kinshasa (then Leopoldville) but found that he could not escape the call. Due to lack of success in that city, he had to return to his own town of N'Kamba. On 6 April 1921 (which is seen today as the date of the founding of the church) Simon reluctantly began a ministry of healing. Soon crowds were flocking to N'Kamba to be healed, and to hear the preaching of salvation through Jesus Christ.

The impact of the preaching and miracles was such that vast numbers came to N'Kamba leading to neglect of the plantations and to the authorities taking an interest. They were afraid of the prophetic movement developing around Kimbangu causing an uprising. They called a meeting of all missionaries who were happy to denounce the new movement. On 6 June 1921 an attempt was made to arrest Kimbangu but this met with resistance, and a state of emergency was proclaimed. Because of a voice from God, Simon allowed himself to be arrested. He was accused of sedition and hostility to whites and was sentenced to death. The missionaries had accepted the ruling of the court, but there were some questions in the minds of the civil authorities and the sentence was commuted to life imprisonment by King Albert. He was transported and spent the remainder of his life in prison until he died in 1951. The active ministry as the prophet was a mere five months.

---

[1] M-L. Martin, *Kimbangu. An African Prophet and his Church* (Basil Blackwell, Oxford, 1975).

From 1921 to 1957 the church was persecuted. In fact the church did not exist as a separate organization, and there were unclear lines between the Kimbanguists and other prophetic groups. It is estimated that 37,000 heads of families were banished, but this process of banishment only helped to spread the movement. There was severe persecution in 1925 but the period 1934-36 was a time of revival associated with the ministry of the Salvation Army. The church was an unofficial part of the Protestant Churches until 1956, when Kimbanguists were ejected from the Mission Churches and were forced to form their own organization. The onset of independence enabled the Kimbanguists to obtain freedom from religious persecution.

In 1957 the church was granted toleration, and in 1959 it was officially recognized and was therefore able to make a statement of its position. While the church had been undergoing persecution there had been no official leadership, but now the prophet's son Joseph Diangienda became head of the church. The church was forced to regularize all the patterns of worship and to train pastors, whereas previous to 1957 the church had been a movement that had taken refuge in the missions and had participated in their life and worship.

The Kimbanguist church building is

'extremely austere . . . [and] those officiating do not wear special dress . . . The service is largely Protestant in type . . . [but] is essentially communal. Everyone takes part in it and it is when the community really lives . . . The festive atmosphere is enhanced by the palm leaves that the people like to wave above their heads'.[1]

People take off the shoes as they enter the church or for any prayer. Also purses, watches and other objects are removed in order to be poor before the Lord. There is daily morning and evening prayer, and members are expected to pray if possible at noon. The morning prayer includes prayers for those who have died in the night, for example 'as Mama Mwilu comes to Thee we pray that Thou accept her'. Wednesday is a special day when no work should be done, and the members should gather for a prayer meeting. The services are long by western standards, but they are full of life—although dancing is not permitted.

Besides the holy communion, baptism, marriage and ordination are regarded as sacraments. The first baptisms were performed in 1957. The service is held twice a year and is performed with Mark 1.8 as the controlling text. The rite is done without water. The candidates kneel before the pastor who takes them by the hand, invokes the name of the Trinity and raises them to their feet.[2] This action is regarded as baptism. Although baptism is dry, water has an important role in healing. Part of the answer to this apparent paradox may be due to the fact that the Salvation Army had a strong impact on many Kimbanguists in the era of persecution. Baptism is regarded as the time when the candidate receives the Holy Spirit. It is through being united with Christ through the Holy Spirit that a person receives the forgiveness of sins.

---

[1] 'The Kimbanguist Church in the Congo' in *Ecumenical Review*, 19 (Jan. 67), pp.31-32.
[2] M-L. Martin, 'Worship and Spirituality in the Kimbanguist Church' in an unpublished paper for a seminar at SOAS, 1974, p.5.

Holy water is used in many contexts for blessing and healing. People use the water daily on themselves, and to bless houses or cars. The water is obtained from the well at N'Kamba which is regarded as a holy well. Indeed N'Kamba has become a place of pilgrimage. It is the New Jerusalem for the church, an anticipation of the glory and peace to come. A pilgrimage there is expected of all Kimbanguists. It is the place where there was a new outpouring of the Holy Spirit in 1921, and it is the place of the burial of the prophet. Water is collected from the well there but also the earth of N'Kamba is taken home.

Kimbanguists have a distinct ending to their prayers; 'In the name of the Father and of the Son and of the Holy Spirit, who has, spoken to us through [or descended on] Simon Kimbangu'. This has caused a certain amount of controversy and it would seem certain that the role of Kimbangu has been one of a messiah or god in the minds of some of the members. Diangienda however sees the role of Simon as comparable to the saints in the Catholic Church:

'Although the Kimbanguist as a Christian has no need of intermediaries, to convey his woes and supplications to Christ by prayer, he can solicit the special aid let us say of Saint Paul, Saint Peter and above all of Simon Kimbangu so that they may support his case with Christ ... Simon Kimbangu ... is an advocate on our behalf with Christ.'[1]

Africans feel a strong unity with their departed. For us they are dead and gone, but for Africans they are dead and still around. Kimbanguists, although essentially Protestant in origin, have here a more 'catholic' theology and practice.

The eucharist did not play an important part in the church at first and there was some caution about how it should be introduced. The primary significance of the eucharist is seen in:

'that the Lord Jesus Christ once more humbles himself by coming to dwell in the being of the communicant ... at the same time forgives the sinner his/her faults. It is one of the very rare moments at which the human being almost attains sanctification, for at the precise moment at which a person receives communion, he or she is united with Christ. By this union the contrite sinner ... benefits from the sanctity of Christ who is present.'[2]

This may seem to be receptionist but the book of services says,

'Le superviseur fait la prière afin que les gâteau et le miel soient transformés par le Seigneur en corps et sang du Christ'.[3]

Thus there is a doctrinal emphasis on the transformation of the elements in the lex orandi and there is no receptionism with the Kimbanguists.

'After the prayer of benediction, the honey and cake become in reality the Body and Blood of Christ. To receive communion ... is very much more than to remember Christ; it is really and truly to eat and drink the Body and Blood of the Lord.'[4]

---

[1] K. J. Diangienda, 'Essence de la théologie Kimbanguist' in *Christian Theology and Strategy for Mission* (Lutheran World Federation, Geneva, 1980), p.231.

[2] *Ibid.*, pp.236.

[3] K. J. Diagienda, *Liturgical Ceremonies of the Church of Jesus Christ on earth through the Prophet Simon Kimbangu*, (Kinshasa, 14 Mai 1974), p.2.

[4] P. Manicom, *Out of Africa—Kimbanguism*, (CEM Student Theology Series, 1979) p.40.

The emphasis is on the sacrament as a rite of sanctification in which Christ comes to dwell in the believer, who is united to Christ. This is the reason for the intense spiritual preparation that Kimbanguists are expected to perform before they receive the sacrament. This includes vigils, retreats, confession of sin, so that 'at the moment of communion the Lord may be welcomed into a "house" which has been put in order as far as possible'.[1] Weekly communion would not enable this intense preparation. One has to be as holy as possible before receiving; it is a table for saints rather than sinners. Once again the passage of Paul in 1 Corinthians 11 is explicitly mentioned.[2]

The Kimbanguists were an offshoot of the Baptists and were much influenced by the Salvation Army. Protestant missions in Zaire tended to use white bread and grenadine syrup as elements for communion.[3] There was much discussion by the church as to the correct elements to use:

'Bread is not indigenous to Central Africa, and no vines grow nearby. Moreover all alcoholic drinks . . . are condemned by the Church.'[4]

It was not until 6 April 1971 that the church first celebrated the communion after there had been five years of discussion on the correct way that it should be done. The foods chosen were a cake made of maize, potatoes and bananas, and a drink made from honey and water. Luntadila explained it this way,

'the foods used to make the elements are found in Zaire and the neighbouring countries. In order to be obedient to the spirit of the Gospel our church has chosen African foods, just as Christ in his day used bread and wine, the daily foods of Palestine'.[5]

The concept of daily food is seen as the important factor rather than the use of the identical materials. This argument contrasts with Cyprian who said that it was necessary not only to be faithful to the spirit of the gospel but also to the original event. We do what the Lord did.

For wine the church uses honey and water. Honey is seen as having Biblical roots in the manna tasting of honey (Ex. 16.31), and Psalm 81.16 is seen to provide a parallel between honey and blood: 'But you would be fed with the finest wheat; with honey from the rock I would satisfy you.' This is an example of analogical logic, which is a common form of classification.[6] From Psalm 81.16 the following form of classification is set up:

wheat : honey
bread : wine
cakes : honey-water
body : blood

---

[1] K. J. Diangienda, 'Essence . . .', p.236.
[2] *Ibid.*, p.237.
[3] Congo Church News, 'Kimbanguist Communion' in *Congo Church News* (April/June 1971) p.25.
[4] M-L. Martin, 'Congolese Church Celebrates' in *Pro Veritate*, 10 (June 1971), pp.4-5.
[5] M-L. Martin, *Kimbangu,* p.180.
[6] R. Neeham, *Reconnaissances,* (University of Toronto Press, Toronto, Buffalo and London, 1980), pp.41-62.

The categories are held together by a set of sporadic resemblances. But, as in all forms of analogic classification, a form of logic is built up:

> honey : rock
> rock : water
> water : wine
> wine : blood

The connection of rock and water is common in the Old Testament. Water and wine are combined in the miracle of Jesus, who also linked wine and blood. Thus it is entirely logical to substitute honey-water for wine.

A further justification is found in the fact that John the Baptist ate honey and that it is full of nourishment. The link to the Baptist is used to justify the idea that honey is 'the food which encouraged meditation, prayer and purity'.[1] This is then confirmed by the fact that the monks of the Ethiopian Orthodox Church use honey, Luntadila continues to argue for the validity of honey on the ground of Luke 24.42 which in some texts has Jesus eating honey rather than fish at this resurrection appearance. The transformation of the pollen by the bee is seen as an illustration of the necessity of inward transformation by the Holy Spirit. Finally it is argued that the bee is an ancient Egyptian symbol, and as such is a profoundly African symbol.

It is significant that these arguments are African-centred. The use of the Ethiopian Orthodox Church as an authority provides an African Christian rationale. That this Church does *not* use honey in the eucharist is irrelevant to Luntadila. The important thing is that there is an African justification—as is seen in the use of the bee, for the bee in Egypt was not a Christian symbol but a pagan one. It is ironic that a church which rejects traditional religion ends up justifying the substitution of honey for wine in the eucharist by referring to an Egyptian pagan symbol. The logic used suggests the primacy of the motif 'daily bread' and that this is interpreted as meaing 'African staple'. Thus the analogical classification can be extended:

> wheat : honey
> bread : wine
> cake : honey-water
> foreign food : African food
> European : African
> colonialist : indigenous
> mission : independent
> missionary : Kimbangu

The set of dyads from the political sphere strengthens the choice of local foods. Indeed the whole *raison d'être* of the church is tied up with the persecution of Kimbangu by the colonialists and the missionaries.

The use of a cake made of maize, bananas and potatoes is justified on the grounds that 'maize and potatoes have saved millions in the world'.[2] The mixing

---

[1] M-L. Martin, *Kimbangu*, p.180.
[2] *Ibid.*, p.181.

of the ingredients shows that the church is a mixture of all the races and the spread of the potato from America is a sign of the need to spread the gospel over all the world. In these arguments no direct reference is made to the life of Jesus and the events of the Last Supper. Rather the logic rests on an allegorical interpretation of the matter used in making the cakes.

The Kimbanguists have developed their own justification for the elements used. This is African theology in the making. The primary motif of 'daily' = 'African' food results in the particular materials used being unique to Kimbanguists. The church is a poor one without the links of the Mission Churches to the West, and thus has less chance of donations from a parent or sister body to enable the import of foreign material (wheat and wine). It is also a church that has received persecution from the state with the acceptance of this by the missions. Therefore it is hardly surprising that the solution to the problem of what to use did not follow the pattern of those organizations from which it had broken away.

The first eucharist was in 1971 at N'Kamba and the consecration was done at the tomb of the prophet. The elements were born in solemn procession to the people by ministers clad in white garments. The cakes were put on simple wooden platters and the wine was put in individual cups. As there were 350,000 pilgrims and 100,000 were eligible for communion, the celebration took thirty-six hours.

The normal order of service is:

1 Sermon.
2 Prayer for transformation of the elements.
3 Procession of the elements to the faithful.
4 Prayers from pastor in the serving team.
5 Reading from 1 Cor. 11.13-29.
6 Two prayers by pastors.
7 Prayer of benediction by the president with hands held in 'orans' position.
8 Reception, the people first and the serving team last.
9 Final common prayer by the president.

There are no set prayers in the service but there are directions at 2, to pray for the elements, and at 7, to pray that Jesus would come and share the sacrament with his church as he did at the Last Supper.

The Kimbanguist Church thought very carefully about the introduction of communion, and has developed a unique form of service—not least in the materials used. Indeed for a church that has its roots in the Baptist Church and the Salvation Army, there is a strong departure from these traditions both in theology and in worship. Part of this must be seen in the unique origins of the movement. The question as to the role of the living dead has been forced by the honour given to Kimbangu, and this question is on the agenda of the other churches in Africa. A whole new symbolic structure has developed in the church, although dry baptism seems to be a surprise, when water is so important in other contexts. Perhaps anthropology comes to particular help in the interpretation of the justification of the elements used for the eucharist. The logic used at first seems strange until it is realized that it rests on a different form of classification— analogical classification—a method that we all use from time to time.

INDEPENDENT CHURCHES: ADAPTATIONS TO AFRICA

The Independent Churches that have been studied have developed their own symbol-systems and services for the eucharist. They have tended to confirm the grid-group theory of Douglas, in that the symbol of the eucharist as transported to Africa has been enriched by the Independent Churches through the addition of a number of secondary symbols (as might be expected from the theory). These churches also seem to be more 'realistic' in their theology of the eucharist, and do not shrink from asking in their prayers for the transformation of the elements into the body and blood of Christ. In a society that is used to taboos, the eucharist is in danger of becoming a rite for the pure due to a 'magical' interpretation of 1 Corinthians 11. It therefore needs to be surrounded by rituals of purification. The orectic pole also is a point of debate in the Independent experience.

It has only been possible to look at two examples and there are many others often unrecorded. As breakaway movements there is the possibility of the production of their own style of worship, one no longer constrained by faithfulness to a tradition. The Independent Churches show one direction of the process of inculturation. They are not an institution trying to inculturate a service, but individuals forming movements of authentically African experience. The Mission Churches could have one eye on these movements when they come to plan their own inculturation.

4. Mission Churches

The African Independent Churches have blazed one trail for authentically African worship and form one of the spurs for Mission Churches towards the indigenization of their worship. But they are not the only factor; others include the pastoral problems of liturgies that do not fit the context (e.g. the contrasting funeral and marriage customs of Africa and Europe), the African theology debate (which is integrated with the discussion of African worship), and the impact of the Liturgical Movement on the sending Churches, who no longer follow the set forms as earlier sent to Africa. There have been some tendencies among Churches in the Anglican Communion, for example, to copy the parent body, as, e.g. those who look to England adopting the ASB, or parts of it, and those who look to America deriving services from the American Book of Common Prayer. This however seems to be the continuation of dependency, a kind of liturgical neo-colonialism. There have been however a few attempts to produce African rites and it is to these that this monograph will now turn. The Roman Catholic Church in particular has invested considerable time in adapting the liturgy and provides a good starting point.

VATICAN TWO

The issue of inculturation was put on the agenda by the Second Vatican Council. One of the first documents to be produced was *Sacrosanctum Concilium* reforming the worship of the church. In the revision of the liturgy, provision is made for local variation and for more radical change. Local variation is permitted in the rubrics of the new services and episcopal conferences have used a few of the possible variations. The Council however cautiously suggests the possibility of local rites that would be different from the Roman rite.

'In some places and circumstances, however, an even more radical adaptation of the liturgy is needed, and this entails greater difficulties . . . the competent ecclesiastical authority ... must in this matter, carefully and prudently consider which elements from the traditions and cultures of the individual peoples might appropriately be admitted into divine worship. Adaptations . . . should then be submitted to the Holy See, by whose consent they may be introduced.'[1]

The Apostolic See will then grant a period of experimentation. Such experimentation has only occurred in two cases in Africa, the Ndzon-Melen Mass and the Zaire Mass. At the same time there have been unofficial documents discussing possible directions.

---

[1] A. Flannery, *Vatican Council II. The Conciliar and Post Conciliar Documents* (Fowler Wright Books Ltd., Leominster, 1975), section 40, p.14.

The Council was cautious about adaptation. It wanted to postulate the 'nut-and-kernel' model, the kernel of the liturgy being given by divine revelation and the nut being the packaging that is culturally conditioned.
'The liturgy is made up of unchangeable elements divinely instituted, and elements subject to change. These latter not only may be changed but ought to be changed . . .'[1]
It is not clear that this is a particularly helpful model for it becomes impossible in reality to distinguish the two. The whole of the rite is the expression of a particular culture. It shows more the grasp of divine revelation by a particular society than the timeless expression of the revelation itself.

The African bishops were not happy with the 'adaptation' metaphor of Vatican Two and suggested that a more radical term be used; not adaptation, but incarnation. In 1974 their synod declared:
'Our theological thinking must remain faithful to the authentic tradition of the Church and, at the same time, be attentive to the life of our communities and respectful of our traditions and languages, that is of our philosophy of life . . . The Bishops of Africa and Madagascar consider as being completely out-of-date, the so-called theology of adaptation. In its stead, they adopt the theology of incarnation. The young churches of Africa cannot refuse to face up to this basic demand.'[2]
The bishops have found it more difficult in practice to go along this road than they may have originally hoped.

UNOFFICIAL INITIATIVES
The passing of *Sacrosanctum Concilium* encouraged the production of a number of private suggestions for liturgical reform. Aylward Shorter wrote four eucharistic prayers which were published in AFER, an East African Catholic Journal.[3] These prayers were adaptations of prayers from African Traditional Religion put together to form an anaphora. Eugene Uzukwu also produced a suggested prayer for the Igbo in Nigeria, also published in AFER.[4] This is perhaps a more satisfactory prayer than those of Shorter but in both cases they are no more than private suggestions and had no official backing (although they may have been used illegally from time to time).

One text that has only recently come to light is the proposed liturgy for Tanzania. The bishops of that country decided to ask some students and staff of a seminary to produce a text with a view to proposing an authorized Tanzanian rite. The project was never completed, but a text was produced and this provides some insights to the way future revision might go.

---

[1] *Ibid.,* §21, p.9.
[2] E. E. Uzukwu, *Liturgy, Truly Christian, Truly African* (Spearhead no. 74, Gaba Publications, Eldoret, Kenya, 1982) pp.27-28.
[3] A. Shorter, 'An African Eucharistic Prayer' in *AFER,* 12 (1970) pp.143-148; A. Shorter, 'Three more African Eucharistic Prayers' in *AFER,* 15 (1973) pp.152-160.
[4] E. E. Uzukwu, 'Blessing and Thanksgiving among the Igbo (Nigeria). Towards an African Eucharistic Prayer' in *AFER,* 7 (1980) p.17.

The rite makes the attempt to be African both in style and in content. Many of the prayers are said responsorially and the phrases used are selected to speak in a Tanzanian context.

The eucharistic prayer begins with an extended thanksgiving for creation: 'O God our Creator ... you created us differently from all other created things—those that are alive and those that are without life ...

'You have blessed us with a beautiful land with valleys and mountains, rivers and lakes, thickets and haunts of wild animals.'[1]

The purpose of this blessing is not, however, for selfish enjoyment but, 'in order that we can use all these things to build a good society'.[2] This would seem to express Tanzanian socialism, and further such expressions are found in the prayer. Thus sin is talked about in these terms:

'many times when we seek to do this [attain perfection] we follow the path of profiting ourselves, not bringing to each one in our community.'[3]

One of the results of the coming of Christ is:

'He has shown us that if we volunteer and serve others in our society even to the point of being ready to give up our lives ... we are building blessedness and your loving intentions in our midst.'[4]

The expression to 'volunteer' in particular would have strong political connotations. Tanzania has had a strong socialist tradition through the long presidency of Nyerere. This is socialism with an African face, emphasizing the importance of brotherhood. There is also a strong Christian component in it, Nyerere being a very devout Catholic. The prayer is one of the few examples of the integration of the religious system and the political in contemporary Africa.

There are also links to traditional religion. The elements are offered 'together with our brothers—our fathers of old, whom you took into your house'.[5] Also in the introduction to the Sanctus the following is said:

'we beseech you that our praises and thanksgivings may unite us with all our *wahenga* and all who praise you ...'[6]

The *wahenga* is a technical term for the elder who leads the ritual of initiation. In Tanzania experiments were made for the Christianization of initiation rites.[7] Thus a Christian *jando* (circumcision ceremony) was created that was acceptable to all concerned. This experiment was begun by the Anglicans and was taken up by the Catholics and continues in some areas even to the present. The importance of the initiation rite to Africans is acknowledged in this prayer which does not seem to discern between traditional and Christianized initiation.

---

[1] A. Shorter, 'Liturgical Creativity in East Africa' in *AFER*, 5 (1977) p.8.
[2] *Ibid.*, p.8.
[3] *Ibid.*, p.8.
[4] *Ibid.*, p.9.
[5] *Ibid.*, p.10.
[6] *Ibid.*, p.9.
[7] V. W. Lucas, *Christianity and Native Rites*, (Central Africa House Press, London, 1950).

This semi-official prayer and the prayers of Shorter and Uzukwu point to a number of issues; the selection of metaphors that are appropriate for Africa in prayer, the position of the ancestors, the relationship between the leaders and the congregation, and the expression of this in the text. Many however who read these texts may find that there is not a clear enough division between Christianity and Traditional Religion. This is due in part to an adoption of Rahner's theology of the anonymous Christian.[1]

THE NDZON-MELEN MASS

In the parish of St. Paul de Ndzon-Melen, Yaounde, Cameroon, there is an official experimental Mass. This began with the encouragement of local music in 1958. Ten years later Fr. Ngumu was appointed to the parish and the Ndzon-Melen Mass was approved one year later.[2] It is one of the earliest experiments in incarnating liturgy.

The Mass has been reorganized around the pattern of the Beti assembly (*etógán*).[3] This assembly is a rite called by any member of the tribe, when they have a particular problem. There are two parts to the gathering. Firstly the people assemble and the problem is discussed. The convener informs those who have come as to the issues involved, and the deliberations begin. There is much interaction between all parties and, when all have had their say, they respond by acclamations to the Ndzo who sums up the discussion. The second part is a communal meal. The significance of this is twofold; gratitude to those who have come to help the afflicted, and a fellowship meal.

The traditional Roman Mass did not tell the people why there was an assembly and had a particular dichotomy between the people and the priest. These elements were perceived to be particularly alien, and thus the Mass was reorganized along the lines of the *etógán*.[4] The two halves of the assembly are similar to the two halves of the Mass. Thus the ministry of the word is reorganized to the pattern of the discussion, and the ministry of the eucharist along the lines of the communal meal. There is no new text but rather the reordering of the service and the development of appropriate symbolic action to accompany it. The order is as follows[5]:

The acclamation of the book.
1   Vesting, singing, dancing.
2   Censing of the book.
3   Procession.
4   Enthronement of the book.
5   Introduction by the commentator.
6   Old Testament Lesson, followed by a song.
7   New Testament Lesson, followed by a song.

[1] K. Rahner, *Theological Investigations* 6 (DLT, London, 1969) pp.390-398.
[2] E. E. Uzukwu, *Liturgy. Truly Christian. Truly African*, p.56.
[3] P. Abega, 'Liturgical Adaptation' in E. Fasholé-Luke (et. al.), *Christianity in Independent Africa* (Rex Collins, London, 1978) p.601.
[4] E. E. Uzukwu, *Liturgy. Truly Christian. Truly African*, p.56.
[5] P. Abega, 'Liturgical Adaptation', pp.602-604.

8   Gospel, and song of meditation.
9   Homily, in dialogue form.
10 Sung Credo and offerings are collected.
11 Reflection and song of supplication.
12 Collect of the day, to conclude the first part.
Communion Meal.
1   Offerings are taken to the altar in a dance.
2   Preface.
3   Sanctus, with dancing.
4   Consecration, with shouts of ovation and applause.
5   Gloria, now a song of welcome.
6   Continuation of the canon
7   Lord's Prayer.
8   Call on the Lamb of God and the Peace.
9   Communion.
10 Song, purification of the vessels, final collect of the people.
11 Blessing of the people and dismissal.

The acclamation of the book reflects the discussion of the assembly. The commentator explains the reason for the assembly. The book is one of the participants speaking to those who have gathered. Great scope is given to response by the people not only in the songs but also in the homily.[1] Elements that do not fit into this pattern have been removed from this section, for example the Gloria and the penitential material. Dance has been included throughout the service as a form of expression of joy. The communion meal is in the order of the traditional Mass except for the Gloria which now functions as a welcome song to the Lord after the consecration of the elements. This has the desired effect of giving this part of the service a greater degree of participation. But this does not fit into the assembly scheme, for presumably by this time all the participants would have been welcomed.

Furlong has criticized the service saying
'there seems to have been no sound liturgical reason for the transposition of the introductory prayers, except the desire to make the Mass conform to the Beti assembly'.[2]
This seems to miss the point. The sound liturgical reason is the inculturation of the liturgy, as encouraged by the Church. But another comment of his reflects the problem raised by the indigenization issue in all Mission Churches:
'the needs of a particular community are considered primary, rather than the needs of the universal Church and the transmitted body of tradition . . . to be truly "Catholic", there must be a recognizably "common" element in all rites'.[3]

---

[1] Cf. A. Shorter, *African Culture and the Christian Church* (Geoffry Chapman, London and Dublin, 1973) pp.104-106.
[2] P. J. Furlong, 'Catholic Initiatives in the Africanisation of Christianity' in *Journal of Theology for Southern Africa*, 43 (June 1983) p.30.
[3] *Ibid.*, p.31.

Indigenization can cause tension in an intercultural church. However it would be naive to equate the European expression of Christianity with the true tradition or the pure Catholic element. The Latin Mass both in word and ceremonial was an adaptation to the needs of the church in the post-Constantine era as revised through a succession of councils. Fidelity to tradition can be seen as faithfulness, not to the forms of a particular era, but to the principle of adaptation, the concretization of the gospel in a particular culture at a particular time.

Chima comments that this is an attempt

'at genuine creativity . . . it is not just a matter of throwing a few African cultural elements into a liturgy that still remains Roman and Western, but rather to give the whole liturgy an "African face and flesh", even if this means reshuffling some of the structural elements of the Mass'.[1]

This Mass has been most radical in the structure of the service but has not produced a distinct text. The liturgical style is distinct with a stress on greater mobility with a heightening of processions and dancing; but in order to find a completely African rite one has to look to Zaire.

THE ZAIRE MASS

The church in Zaire grasped the opportunity presented by the Second Vatican Council and began in 1969 to research into a new rite. The policies of president Mobutu may have made them particualrly sensitive to the issue. By 1972 they had completed their research and the experimental rite received approval.

The principles of the rite are 'fidelity to the values of the gospel; fidelity to the essential nature of the Catholic liturgy; and fidelity to the religious and cultural heritage of Zaire.'[2] Thus the eucharistic prayer is based on that of Hippolytus but at the same time the service has freely adapted parts of tradition. 'What underlies the whole rite is . . . a search for "authenticity": and authenticity that is truly Christian and truly African'.[3] Thus the assembly begins with the atmosphere of gathering as if to visit a chief. The atmosphere is one of expectancy. The messenger announces that the celebration is about to start and the song begins. Attention has been paid to all aspects of the service. Music has been composed locally. The vestments used are the ceremonial wear of chiefs (it is worth contrasting this with the stole, a garment that had its origin in secular use, that of the magistrate in the Roman empire). Dance is an integral part of the service. The text includes many acclamations, concrete images, repetitions and gestures. The full text of the Mass has been reproduced in English by Thurian and Wainwright.[4]

The service begins with the invocation of the saints. Before coming into the presence of the Holy, the ancestors who are closer to the deity are called upon to

[1] A. Chima, 'Africanizing the Liturgy—Where are we 20 years after Vatican 2' in *AFER*, 25 (1984), p.283.

[2] B. Hearne, 'The significance of the Zaire Mass' in *AFER*, 17 (1975) pp.216-217.

[3] *Ibid., p.217.*

[4] M. Thurian and G. Wainwright (Eds.), *Baptism and Eucharist: Ecumenical Convergence in Celebration* (WCC, Eerdmans, Grand Rapids, 1983) pp.205-209.

be present. After the invocation of Mary and the patron, the litany continues:

Celebrant. Holy people of heaven, be with us: you who see God; here is our prayer: be with us, and all who celebrate this mass at this time.

People. **Be with us, be with us all.**

Celebrant. And you, our ancestors, be with us, you who have served God with a good conscience, be with us. Here is our prayer: be with us, and all who celebrate mass at this time

People. **Be with us, be with us all.**[1]

This reflects a liturgical attempt to grapple with both the traditional approach to the ancestors and the Christian doctrine of the communion of the saints.

In the Gloria the faithful dance in their places and the ministers dance around the altar—a sign of joy at the coming voice of the holy. For the collect all raise their hands—a sign of oneness of the hearts of all as they pray together. The acclamation of the Gospel reflects the tradition of the people listening to the storyteller, hence people sit to listen:

C. The Good News, as Saint N. has written it

P. **Announce it, announce it, we are listening.**

After the reading:

C. He who has ears to hear

P. **Let him hear!**

C. He who has a heart to receive

P. **Let him receive!**[2]

The penitential rite is put after the Creed and before the intercessions, as a 'ceremony of ritual reintegration'[3] after confrontation with the word of God. This is a strange interpretation. Reintegration in Turner's model is at the end of a rite. Here it would seem to be viewed as a response of penitence to the reading and homily which is assumed by Uzukwu to be confrontational. It would be a better interpretation to see its positional meaning as purification for the coming presence of the holy in the sacred meal.

Concrete imagery is used in the litany of confession:

'Lord our God, like the insect that sticks onto our skin and sucks our blood, evil has come upon us. Our living power is weakened . . .'

and in the absolution:

'May your Spirit take possession of our hearts, and may our sins be drowned in the deep and silent waters of your mercy'.

During the prayers 'the people express their sorrow by taking up, an attitude of repentance: 'head slightly bowed, arms crossed on the breast'.[4] The people are sprinkled with holy water and the sign of peace is exchanged.

---

[1] *Ibid.,* p.205.
[2] *Ibid.,* p.206.
[3] E. Uzukwu, *Liturgy. Truly Christian. Truly African,* p.62.
[4] M. Thurian and G. Wainwright, *Baptism and Eucharist,* pp.206-207.

The eucharistic prayer follows the norms of the Roman rite in that it follows the same structural outline, but uses African imagery and is responsorial in style. The praise of God in the preface uses 'images which characterize traditional African experience of God':[1]

You, 'sun too bright for our gaze',
You, the allpowerful
You, the all seer,
You, the Master of men
You, Master of life,
You, Master of all things . . .
through Jesus Christ the one who is our mediator with you.
Yes, he is our mediator!

God is praised for Christ, the agent of creation in the world that is seen:

Through him, you created heaven and earth,
Through him, you created our river, the Zaire.
Through him, you created our forests, our rivers, our lakes.
Through him you have created all things!

Then thanks is given for the saving acts of the Son.

In the Narrative of Institution a drum or gong is gently beaten, emphasizing the presence of the holy in the same way as do the traditional bells. The text at this point continues its responsorial nature and therefore includes acclamations:

This is my body which will be given up for you.
This is your Body; we believe. . . .
This is the cup of my blood . . .
This is your Blood; we believe.

The service continues with the Roman rite of communion and ends with the traditional Roman rite of post-communion, but expressed in joyful dancing.

Hearn concluded that, while

'the "Zaire Mass" can scarcely be called sensational or radical in its innovations, it represents a big step forward in that it points the way to a possible "African Rite" in the not too distant future.'[2]

Uzukwu's view is that it is

'a genuine effort to translate the local Church's faith-experience into ritual. They have succeeded in making a translation which keeps the Zairean world, with all its dynamism, in a healthy dialogue tension with the living Jewish-Christian tradition'.[3]

But the Pope in a recent visit to Zaire refused to celebrate this liturgy. He commented to the Zairean bishops on their visit to Rome that

'a liturgy corresponding to the soul of African culture cannot be realized except as the result of a progressive maturation of the faith.'[4]

---

[1] E. Uzukwu, *Liturgy. Truly Christian. Truly African,* p.64.
[2] B. Hearne, 'The significance of the Zaire Mass', p.219.
[3] E. Uzukwu, *Liturgy. Truly Christian. Truly African,* p.65.
[4] M. Kane, 'African Liturgy and the Papal Visit to Zaire' in *AFER,* 26 (1984), p.246.

The caution of the authorities that this symbolizes has led to frustration in the church. Kane commented

'Does it really need 400 or 500 years, as the Pope seems to suggest, in order to find authentic expression?'[1]

CHURCH OF THE PROVINCE OF KENYA

The Anglican Church in Kenya (CPK) after many years of being devoutly 1662 has produced a proposed eucharistic liturgy. This is a fine example of African worship. Unlike most other products of the liturgical movement it takes its starting point from the present texts of the church, the 1662 Book of Common Prayer, and transforms this service in an African direction.

A number of sources have been drawn on for inculturating the service. There is a cautious use of material from African Traditional Religion. In the intercessions a litany is developed that is based on a Kikuyu litany. The final blessing is also based on a Turkana blessing.

> *Minister:* All our problems
> *People:* **We send to the setting sun.**
> *Minister:* All our difficulties
> *People:* **We send to the setting sun.**
> *Minister:* All the devil's works
> *People:* **We send to the setting sun.**
> *Minister:* All our hopes
> *People:* **We set on the Risen Son.**

This is followed with an Anglican blessing, and is accompanied with sweeping of the arm to the west and, for the last response, to the east.

There is also a cautious inclusion of the ancestors. One of the introductions to prayer says, 'Let us pray to the God of our fathers, through Jesus Christ his Son'. Thanks are given for 'our Christian ancestors . . . [may] we walk in their footsteps'. The sanctus is introduced with the words 'with angels and archangels, and Christian ancestors in heaven'.[2]

Metaphors used to describe God are carefully chosen to relate to African culture. God is called Creator of the living and the non-living, Great Elder, Allocator, great Father. Jesus is called 'our Brother' and 'your First Born'. Thus the post-communion prayer is a new production:

> 'Almighty God, our great Elder,
> we have sat at your feet,
> learnt from your word,
> and eaten at your table.
> We give you thanks and praise
> for accepting us into your family.
> Send us out with your blessing,
> to live and witness to you
> in the power of your Spirit,
> through Jesus Christ, your First Born.
> Amen.'

---

[1] *Ibid.*, p.247.
[2] The eucharistic prayer of this draft rite is set out in full in the Appendix on page 43 below.

The choice of metaphors has become a live issue both in the west and in Africa. In the west the feminist liturgists are raising questions about the choice of language, not least in the question why, if the Bible includes the use of feminine metaphors for God they are excluded from liturgical revision? Likewise in Africa, the question is, why not use metaphors that speak more clearly as, e.g., referring to Jesus as Brother, or God as great Elder?

This newly proposed Kenyan service is an important departure for a Church that so far has been closely faithful to the missionary tradition, and shows a certain maturity in the development of indigenous prayer rather than in the importation of the liturgical revisions of the west.[1]

MISSION CHURCHES AND CULTURE

As might be expected the Mission Churches have tended to be slow in the inculturation of worship. The pull of tradition has been strong both for those churches that espouse tradition and for those that in theory reject it. There is a strong loyalty by the Africans to the tradition as received, that of the gospel and the Prayer Book. But this has also produced the tension of services that are both foreign and also at times incomprehensible in what they say and do. Even in a denomination such as the Anglican Church, which in theory has the possibility of an indigenous rite for each province, there has been a reluctance to transpose the liturgy. This is such that there is a tendency today to look to the parent bodies and introduce their new services, or minor variants on them, rather than produce local rites such as is under way in Kenya. This dependence however will not solve the underlying causes of the cry for indigenization.

The African theology movement is closely linked to the question of inculturated worship. What are the African language games for prayer? Are certain motifs more appropriate in Africa than in the west? What is the notion of sacrifice in the service (an important question in an environment where sacrifices are still common)? How is community expressed in the worship event? Indeed all the aspects of the service that have led to its present form need to be reorientated for a dialogue with African culture.

One of the greatest problems for any intercultural denomination is the question of the relationship between individuality and catholicity. Vatican Two cautiously allowed the possibility of local liturgies. The unifying factor seems to be the authority of the Holy See. In reality the Vatican has been very cautious about the authorization of local rites. The problem is even more acute for the Anglicans, who have all authority delegated to each province. If the Book of Common Prayer ceases to be the norm throughout the Anglican Communion, what is it that holds it together? Anglicans are only just beginning to realize that a

---

[1] For further Anglican discussion of the indigenization of the liturgy see, E. Mbonigaba, 'Indigenization of the Liturgy', in T. J. Talley (ed.), *A Kingdom of Priests: Liturgical Formation of the People of God* (Alcuin/GROW Joint Liturgical Study 5, Grove Books, Bramcote, 1988), pp.39-47. See also *An Experimental Liturgy for Archbishop Janani Luwum Theological College* (Catholic Press, Gulu, 1985).

Communion of one form of worship is in fact a myth that has never existed. Underlying all this is the question of the way authority is to operate in a worldwide denomination, but then Douglas put control at the very centre of her theory as to the relationship between symbol and culture, so perhaps that is not altogether surprising.

The Zaire Mass and the draft Revised Service of Holy Communion of CPK are two important examples of what are here called Mission Churches producing indigenous rites. As such, they are pioneers in the process of inculturation and give the shape of things to come. They both have many things to commend them as an expression of African spirituality, and should not be dismissed as products of some new form of neo-colonialism. The question of inculturation arises not as the result of a set of new theories, whether from the west or from Africa itself, but is a problem arising out of the new cultural context for the eucharist. It is a question of a search for authenticity.

5. Inculturation

This monograph has tried to look at the question of indigenization from the point of view of examining the eucharist in Africa, using the concept of symbol as the guiding metaphor. Perhaps it is now opportune to try to draw some of the threads together and to elucidate more the question at hand. This can be done by examining two issues.

ADEQUACY

In looking at Tillich's doctrine of symbol the concept of adequacy was touched upon. This is a useful concept for the examination of inculturation. A symbol is adequate, if it has the power to express ultimate concern in such a way that it creates reply, action and communication.[1] The call for inculturation occurs, when the power to do this is waning. This may be for a number of reasons, not least 'foreignness' as a result of the cross-cultural transference of symbol. Some symbols transfer easily across cultural barriers. Water for example has become an important symbol in many Independent Churches. It is often connected to baptism but also to healing. Perhaps this is due to the fact that water is a natural symbol and therefore it has a universal appeal: without water there is no life. The eucharist on the other hand relies on products that are manufactured and therefore introduces a greater cultural element to the symbolism. The materials used, wheat and wine, may not relate in a society based on other agricultural complexes. The service surrounding the symbol may reflect the agenda of a church from a different continent. The translation of the text of the Narrative of Institution may require the use of loan words due to a lack of local words for bread and wine. All of this contributes to the foreignness of the eucharistic event.

The churches have responded in a variety of ways to the problem. There has been discussion as to the materials to be used for the bread and the wine. The Kimbanguists are an example of the use of local materials. There is also growing concern for the production of local texts, which reflect the agenda of the African Churches, a searching for metaphors and expressions that resonate in the African context. The Zaire Mass and the new draft rite from the Church of the Province of Kenya are examples of this.

How is a symbol to express itself adequately? Tillich pointed out tha committees are unable in the final analysis to produce symbols. In England the Anglican Church has produced a new service book. In it the taking of the bread and the wine are clearly directed as a compulsory action. Yet this is in fact rarely done. This symbolic action may have been introduced by the authorities but it is not a living reality in the life of the church. Adequacy suggests an interaction between the symbol itself (and perhaps therefore the guardians of the symbol) and the

---

[1] P. Tillich, *Dynamics of Faith* (Allen and Unwin, London, 1957), p.96.

operation of the symbol in the worship event. There is little that can be suggested but the openness of the church authorities and local congregations to experimentation. The goal must be the deepening of the community's eucharistic life.

LITURGICAL THEOLOGY
One of the previous monographs in this series has examined different models for that elusive topic, liturgical theology.[1] Here in the second chapter the approach of Schmemann—*lex orandi lex credendi*—was introduced, and it may seem that it was soon forgotten. However the whole approach of this monograph could be described as the anthropological model for liturgical theology.[2] This model tries to start from the worship event, and then subjects it to symbolic analysis and looks for implicit meanings. Thus it incorporates the approaches of anthropologists and theologians. It may seem that this is an unlikely combination and it may result in unresolved tensions at times, but it may also enrich our understanding and would seem to be necessary in the examination of topics where culture is one of the central components. Inculturation is one such issue.

The development of the social sciences has been seen as a threat to the Christian understanding of God and man. Their rise may seem to have undermined much that was seen to be revealed truth, and our view of man today probably has more to do with Darwin, Marx and Freud than with Paul, Augustine or Aquinas. However, dialogue rather than isolation is the answer. The anthropological model of liturgical theology is one that entails a dialogue both of listening and critique. Thus it can take on board elements from anthropology without being threatened and at the same time be critical of others, not least those which seem to undermine theology altogether. Symbols are of vital importance to the worship of the church. It was part of the genius of Jesus that he did not give us a service book, or a collection of rubrics, but rather two symbols, baptism and the eucharist. Therefore symbolic analysis is vital not only to theology itself, nor only to the language of revelation, but above all to the worship of the church and especially its supreme symbol, that of the eucharist.

---

[1] J. Empereur, *Models of Liturgical Theology*, (Alcuin/GROW Joint Liturgical Study 4, Grove Books, Bramcote, 1987).
[2] See also M. M. Kelleher, 'Liturgical Theology: A Task and a Method' in *Worship*, 62 (1988), pp.2-25.

Appendix: Kenyan Draft Eucharistic Prayer

The text below, to which reference is made in this Study, is simply a draft of the CPK Liturgical Committee released in late 1987. It is subject to further change by the Committee, and then may or may not be authorized for use.

Minister: Is the Father with us?

People: **He is.**

Minister: Is Christ among us?

People: **He is.**

Minister: Is the Spirit here?

People: **He is.**

Minister: Now who is our God?

People: **Father, Son and Holy Spirit.**

Minister: And who are we?

People: **His faithful people.**

Minister: Lift up your hearts.

People: **We lift them to the Lord.**

Minister: Let us give thanks to the Lord our God.

People: **It is right to give him thanks and praise.**

Minister: It is right and our delight
to give you thanks and praise,
great Father, living God,
supreme over the world,
Creator, Allocator,
Saviour and Giver.
From a wandering nomad
you created your family;
for a burdened people
you raised up a leader;
for a confused nation
you chose a king;
for a rebellious crowd
you sent your prophets.
In these last days
you have sent us your Son,
your perfect image,
bringing your kingdom,
revealing your will,
dying, rising, reigning,
remaking your people for yourself.

Through him you have sent upon us
your life-giving Spirit,
filling us with energy and light.

Special Thanksgivings when appropriate
Therefore with angels and archangels,
and Christian ancestors in heaven,
we proclaim your great and glorious name,
forever praising you and saying:

All: **Holy, holy, holy Lord,**
God of power and might,
heaven and earth are full of your glory.
Hosanna in the highest.

Minister: Owner of all things,
We thank you for giving up your only Son
to die on the cross
for us who owe you everything.

Pour your refreshing Spirit on us
as we remember him in the way he commanded,
through these gifts of your creation.

On the same night that he was betrayed
he took bread and gave you thanks;
he broke it gave it to his disciples, saying,
Take, eat; this is my body which is given for you;
Do this in remembrance of me.

People: **Amen. His body was broken for us.**

Minister: In the same way, after supper
he took the cup and gave you thanks;
he gave it to them saying,
Drink this, all of you;
this is my blood of the new covenant,
which is shed for you and for many for the forgiveness of sins.
Do this as often as you drink it,
in remembrance of me.

People: **Amen. We are brothers and sisters through his blood.**
We have died together,
we will rise together,
we will live together.

Minister: Therefore, heavenly Father,
hear us as we celebrate
this covenant with joy,
and await the coming of our Brother.
He died in our place,
making a full atonement
for the sins of the whole world,
the perfect sacrifice, once and for all.
You accepted his offering
by raising him from death,
and granting him great honour
at your right hand on high.

People: **Amen. Jesus is Lord.**

Minister: This is the feast of victory.

People: **The Lamb who was slain has begun his reign.**
Hallelujah.

Alcuin/Grow Joint Liturgical Studies

1987 TITLES

1. **(LS 49) Daily and Weekly Worship—from Jewish to Christian**
   by R. T. Beckwith, Warden of Latimer House, Oxford
   [OUT OF STOCK UNTIL REPRINTED]

2. **(LS 50) The Canons of Hippolytus**
   edited by Paul Bradshaw, Professor of Liturgics, University of Notre Dame
   These Canons, only available in manuscript in Arabic, reflect a Greek original which has been variously dated by scholars, but is here located in the early fourth century. This makes it the earliest source of Hippolytus himself.

3. **(LS 51) Modern Anglican Ordination Rites**
   edited by Colin Buchanan, Bishop of Aston
   The revisions of the last 15 years throughout the Anglican Communion are collected and presented by Colin Buchanan, who has here done for ordination rites what he has done three times in the last decades for eucharistic rites.

4. **(LS 52) Models of Liturgical Theology**
   by James Empereur, of the Jesuit School of Theology, Berkeley
   Worship may be characterized differently, depending on the dominant model at work, such as liturgy as institution, as mystery, as sacrament, as proclamation, as process, as therapeutic, and as liberation. No one model exhausts the meaning of the liturgy; no one model can be omitted from an adequate theological understanding of the worship of the assembly.

NEW—1988 TITLES

5. **(LS 53) A Kingdom of Priests: Liturgical Formation of the Laity: The Brixen Essays**
   edited by Thomas Talley, Professor of Liturgics, General Theological Seminary, New York.
   This volume is a thoroughly edited collection of the salient papers read at the second international Anglican Liturgical Consultation held at Brixen in Northern Italy in August 1987—and, from America, Britain, and Africa alike, they combine planning aspects of the liturgy to-day in Anglicanism with the 'results' in terms of the building up of the laity.

6. **(LS 54) The Bishop in Liturgy: an Anglican Study**
   edited by Colin Buchanan, Bishop of Aston
   This symposium begins from a paper of Colin Buchanan, delivered at the Brixen Consultation but deliberately excluded from Study no. 5 summarized above. Some treatment of history, of pastoral considerations, and of expectations varying from diocese to diocese and continent to continent, leads on into practical help for bishops and for all those who welcome bishops to minister in their parishes or larger contexts.

7. **(LS 55) Inculturation: the Eucharist in Africa**
   by Phillip Tovey, research student, previously tutor in liturgy in Uganda
   The author draws upon broad study and also his own experience in Africa and in Britain to pose the questions and point in a healthful direction for answers, concerning the relating of liturgy to local culture in Africa.

8. **(LS 56) Essays in Early Eastern Initiation** (December 1988)
   edited by Paul Bradshaw, Professor of Liturgics, University of Notre Dame
   A well-known editor from the Church of England, a professor at Notre Dame University, presents three authors who open up new issues and provide new theories in relation to the early Eastern baptismal rites.

Alcuin Club membership is open to all applicants sending £7 (or US$18) to the Alcuin Club, Norton Vicarage, Windmill Hill, Runcorn, Cheshire WA7 6QE. Those who have previously obtained Grove Liturgical Studies on standing order will find it cheaper to join the Alcuin Club (though payment must then be made in advance, rather than arrears), but must notify Grove Books Ltd. at the same time of the cancellation of their Standing Order (or that part of it), or they may be held liable for both.